SYD HOFF'S
ANIMAL
JOKES

SYD HOFF'S
ANIMAL
JOKES

J.B. Lippincott   New York

Library of Congress Cataloging in Publication Data
Hoff, Syd, 1912-
   Syd Hoff's Animal jokes.

   Summary: A collection of jokes, puns, and cartoons
about animals.
   1. Animals—Humor.   2. Wit and humor, Juvenile.
(1. Animals—Wit and humor.   2. Jokes.   3. Wit and humor)
I. Title.   II. Title: Animal jokes.
PN6231.H64 1985   818'.5402   84-48353
ISBN 0-397-32116-3
ISBN 0-397-32117-1 (lib. bdg.)

Designed by Constance Fogler
2 3 4 5 6 7 8 9 10

For the cat and the dog
around the corner

"Tell me the story of Goldilocks."

What did the fish say
when the pelican caught it?

P-OUCH!

What was the bull doing
in the department store?

Charging.

When do squirrels chase people?

When they think they're *nuts.*

What kind of doctor treats a duck?

A *quack* doctor.

"And don't forget the cat food."

"Well, this isn't good weather for *me*!"

"No, he's not in."

"You must have been a beautiful egg."

"Oh, Harry, you shouldn't have!"

"Why, yes, we board pets."

How can you tell
that fish is playing hookey?

It isn't in a school.

What part of a lobster
is popular on Christmas?

Sandy Claws.

Woodpeckers are always tapping on trees.

That sounds boring.

What did one crustacean tell another?

You're a crab.

Do storks really bring babies?

Yes, baby *storks*.

Why wasn't the knight afraid of the dragon?

He had a fire extinguisher.

What kind of fish pray?

Holy mackerel.

Why doesn't your parakeet talk?

We're not on speaking terms.

"I forgot something."

"Charles makes friends wherever he goes."

"I'm from Loch Ness.
Where do *you* come from?"

"You look familiar.

Haven't we met somewhere before?"

"How long did you say
you've done this kind of work?"

"Mrs. Miller,
your dog has just been expelled!"

What kind of worms get married?

*Ring*worms.

What do moose do on New Year's Eve?

They blow their horns.

Why don't frogs live long?

They're always croaking.

Why did the leopard go to a cleaner?

To get its spots removed.

What makes little bears go into a cave?

Their den mother.

What did Blitzen tell Prancer?

You're a deer.

"I'm sorry, there's no Rover here. Why don't you try the doghouse next door?"

"I attacked someone
sneaking into the house at 3 A.M.
My owner."

"How can I get enough to eat when you always get the lion's share?"

"How long has the patient been on goat's milk?"

"Someday they'll probably be extinct."

"Cut your grass, lady?"

"Well, Sam, we can't add,
but we sure can multiply."

"I wish somebody would hurry up and invent a nonfattening tin can."

How long can a camel go without water?

Until it gets thirsty.

What kind of music do monkeys like?

Swing.

"I don't feel well. I must have eaten something that wasn't one hundred percent wool."

7